THOMAS KINKADE

with

Anne Christian Buchanan

Finding a
Peaceful Place

Harvest House Publishers
Eugene, Oregon

Finding a Peaceful Place

Text Copyright © 2002 Thomas Kinkade, Media Arts Group, Inc.,
Morgan Hill, CA 95037 and Harvest House Publishers, Eugene, OR 97402

Published by Harvest House Publishers
Eugene, OR 97402

Library of Congress Cataloging-in-Publication Data
Kinkade, Thomas, 1958-
      Finding a peaceful place / Thomas Kinkade.
         p.cm. – (Simpler times collections)
     ISBN 0-7369-0639-8
     1. Simplicity. 2. Peace of mind. I. Title.

BJ1496 .K55 2002
179'.9–dc21

2001038506

Media Arts Group, Inc.
900 Lightpost Way
Morgan Hill, CA 95037
1.800.366.3733

Text for this book has been excerpted from *Simpler Times* by
Thomas Kinkade (Harvest House Publishers, 1996).

Harvest House Publishers has made every effort to trace the ownership of
all poems and quotes. In the event of a question arising from the use of a
poem or quote, we regret any error made and will be pleased to make the
necessary corrections in future editions of this book.

Verses are taken from the Holy Bible, New International Version®.
Copyright © 1973, 1978, 1984 by the International Bible Society.
Used by permission of Zondervan Publishing House.

Design and production by Koechel Peterson & Associates,
Minneapolis, Minnesota

Printed in Hong Kong

02 03 04 05 06 07 08 09 10 11/ NG / 10 9 8 7 6 5 4 3 2 1

I am beginning to learn that it is the sweet, simple things of life which are the real ones after all.

—LAURA INGALLS WILDER

A separate peace.

It has happened in history for a variety of reasons, honorable and dishonorable. Many countries have enthusiastically gone to war. Banners flying, boots shining, a proud little nation joins the mighty alliance and marches off to war. Eager to defend its honor, it plunges enthusiastically into the fray.

The Lord gives strength to his people;
the Lord blesses his people with peace.

—PSALM 29:11

Thomas
Kinkade

Years later, the banners have grown ragged, and the little nation that marched off so proudly has begun to wonder if the war was really worth it. Perhaps it's time for a separate peace.

Does that scenario sound familiar?

To me, it conjures up images of a lot of people I know. They are weary and discouraged just from trying to keep up with the wars they thought they wanted—the war to get ahead, the war to keep up with others, the war for bigger and better and more and more. It's a battleground offered each day in the modern world.

All the lands are at rest and at peace; they break into singing.

—ISAIAH 14:7

If you don't believe me, just picture the freeway closest to where you live. Or the mall on sale day. Your local McDonald's at lunch hour. A sales meeting in a nearby office.

As far as I can see, "normal" life as we know it is not normal at all. It's not designed to make human life happier or more meaningful or even more productive.

My people will live in peaceful dwelling places, in secure homes, in undisturbed places of rest.

—ISAIAH 32:18

And without even knowing it, perhaps even without wanting to, you find yourself hurling into the fray, without really considering whether you have an option.

But you do.

You may not be able to shut down the war, but you don't have to fight somebody else's battles. You don't have to surrender your sanity to someone else's insanity.

You can choose to make a separate peace, to find a peaceful place.

Cherish your human connections: your relationships with friends and family.

—BARBARA BUSH

A musician must make music, an artist must paint, a poet must write,
if he is to be ultimately at peace with himself. What a man can be, he must be.

—ABRAHAM MASLOW

On a little or a large level, you can make choices that take you away from the battleground. In the process, you will be choosing to live in saner, simpler times.

How do you do it? At the very simplest level, you find a place to retreat. You arrange for a refuge where you can rest and be renewed before returning to the fray. Your corner of peace may be as simple as a comfortable chair with an old-fashioned lamp beside it. You turn on the lamp and sink into the chair in the circle of warm light.

Let us therefore make every effort to do what leads to peace...

—ROMANS 14:19

*Nobody sees a flower really; it is so small. We haven't time,
and to see takes time — like to have a friend takes time.*

—GEORGIA O'KEEFFE

Or your peaceful place can be a book; you turn the pages and step through the word windows into another world. It can be a painting—a painting that pulls you into its vision of beauty, that gives you a picture of what a peaceful world can be.

If I have done the hardest possible day's work, and then come to sit down in a corner and eat my supper comfortably—why, then, I don't think I deserve any reward for my hard day's work—for am I not now at peace? Is not my supper good?

—HERMAN MELVILLE

I hear the yearning for a place to retreat every day from people who talk or write to me about my paintings. "That's where I want to be," they say of a scene I've depicted. "I want to step into that painting, walk down the path, and live in that house with the glowing windows."

Obviously, they don't really want to live in a painting. They are simply desiring the world of peace and simplicity I try to portray in my work. They are yearning for a life that focuses on what is truly important and what is truly beautiful—a life that is different from the rushed, cluttered, existence our popular culture promotes.

Simplicity of life, even the barest, is not a misery, but the very foundation of refinement; a sanded floor and whitewashed walls and the green trees, and flowery meads, and living waters outside.

—WILLIAM MORRIS

I went to the woods because
I wished to live deliberately,
to front only the essential
facts of life, and see if I could
not learn what it had to teach,
and not, when I came to die,
discover that I had not lived.
I did not wish to live what was
not life, living is so dear.

—HENRY DAVID THOREAU

There is nothing wrong with that kind of yearning. It's my yearning, too, and the reason I paint the kind of scenes I do. In fact, I believe something has gone seriously wrong if we don't have that kind of hunger for a better, more peaceful way of life. Human beings were not made for the rush-hour, freeway kind of life we try so frantically to live. We were made for calm, not chaos, and that is why we long for a separate peace. Somewhere deep inside we know that simpler times are better times.

Simplicity is making the journey of this life with just baggage enough.

—CHARLES DUDLEY WARNER

That's the kind of life I strive to evoke in my paintings. It's the kind of life I'm committed to building for myself and my family.

And it's the foundational message I want to share with the world through my work and through my life.

A special room in my studio offers me one of my favorite retreats. It is lined with books by and about my heroes—the artists who feed my spirit and enlarge my horizons. I love to sit in the chair by the window and pore over the beautifully printed monographs, losing myself in the works of the greatest painters who have ever lived. They inspire me, they challenge me, they open up new worlds for me. They also offer me peace.

Life is measured by the number of things you are alive to.

—MALTBIE D. BABCOCK

Another favorite retreat for me is a lawn chair in the small grassy yard outside my studio. In that chair I have perfected the art of taking mini-vacations. Even on my most hectic days I can manage to take fifteen minutes to enjoy a sandwich or pray or doze in the sun—just closing my eyes and drifting.

My own work is a retreat for me as well. I live in my paintings as I work on them, and I deliberately paint scenes that serve as places of refuge for battle-weary people. When I am painting a scene, I am walking down the path, peering around the curve of the river, wondering what's around the bend. I am crossing the bridge, strolling in the sun-dappled shadows, feeling the peace. I have even been known to shiver on a warm summer day while painting a snowy winter scene.

Seek peace and pursue it.

—PSALM 34:14

Your place of retreat, your little corner of peace, may be very different from mine. The specifics don't really matter. The point is you find a place or an activity that gives your senses a chance to unwind and lets you catch a fresh vision of peacetime possibilities. Furnish it comfortably. Make it beautiful. Use it often.

But if a little corner of peace makes such a difference, doesn't it make sense to make larger life choices with an eye to simplicity and peace? Of course it does.

He grants peace to your borders and satisfies you with the finest of wheat.

—PSALM 147:14

I want to say a deep, enthusiastic yes to the work that I am called to do in this world. It's a harmful fallacy that work has to be a source of stress and anxiety and striving and that "getting away from it all" has to mean leaving work behind. But saying yes to my work doesn't mean doing everything I am asked to do or even everything I want to do.

My personal calling at this time of my life, in addition to being an active, caring, involved husband and father, is to create paintings and books that reach out and bless the lives of others. Everything else is peripheral—even important tasks, even things I enjoy or that get me excited.

If the sight of the blue skies fills you with joy, if a blade of grass springing up in the fields has power to move you, if the simple things of nature have a message that you understand, rejoice, for your soul is alive . . .

—ELEONORA DUSE

When I learn to say a deep, passionate yes to the things that really matter—and no to whatever gets in the way of that yes—then the peace begins to settle onto my life like golden sunlight sifting to a forest floor.

And that, I find, is a peace worth fighting for.

A truly great man never puts away the simplicity of a child.

—CHINESE PROVERB

It is always the simple that produces the marvelous.

— AMELIA BARR